What's in the box?

A piece of cheese!

What's in the box?

A mouse!

What's in the box?

A cat!

What's in the box?

Nothing!

Beginning to Read
Titles by Bill Gillham

Two Babies
Illustrated by Adriano Gon

What's in the Box?
Illustrated by Susie Jenkin-Pearce

Dirty Dog
Illustrated by Alan Snow

My Dog's Party
Illustrated by Alan Snow

My Pet
Illustrated by Alan Snow

Guess Who I Am!
Illustrated by Alex Ayliffe

What For?
Illustrated by Alex Ayliffe

Where's Woolly?
Illustrated by Alex Ayliffe

What do the animals find in
the box?

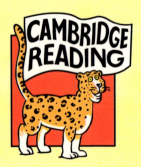

Beginning to Read: A

CAMBRIDGE
UNIVERSITY PRESS

ISBN 0-521-47826-X